Sammy the Centipede Goes to the Market

by **Maria Luchsinger**

Illustrations by
Joe Palmisano

ISBN: 0989763005
EAN-13: 978-0-9897630-0-4

Printed in the U.S.A.

Sammy the Centipede Goes to the Market

by **Maria Luchsinger**

Illustrations by Joe Palmisano

Hi, I'm Sammy
the Centipede.
I love to run
and play.
I do my best
on every test
because I eat
right every day.

Can you find a rainbow
to eat at the market?
As you turn the pages
you will find out.

I love to eat! One day, I noticed my sections were starting to look different. Some of them were getting very large. I did not like the way I looked, and I couldn't move as well as I once could.

I decided to go see my doctor, and he sent me to a dietitian. A dietitian is a person who can help you learn about nutrition and which foods are good for you to eat.

The dietitian said, "Sammy, let's see what you have been eating that has caused this to happen." I told her I loved to snack on candy, soda, and donuts. She said it was okay to eat them sometimes, but most of the time I should eat healthy food because all of these snacks have too much sugar in them.

Sugar tastes so good, so why is too much sugar bad for my body? She said the foods I love are full of sugar that my body uses up very fast and then I feel hungry again. When I keep eating these foods, the sugar feeds the fat that goes to my sections to make them larger.

Sugar makes me think I am full so I don't eat enough foods that I need to keep my body healthy. When I want something sweet, I found out I could eat fruits and foods made with honey. Honey is still sugar, although it is a better choice. Sugar can harm my teeth so I need to remember to brush my teeth after sugary snacks.

After my visit, I learned an easy way to remember how to choose healthy food to keep my body in the right shape. Now when I go to the market, I choose foods that have the colors of the rainbow just like the colors of my body. Red is my favorite color, so I like to think of red fruits and vegetables first.

Healthy Red foods are:

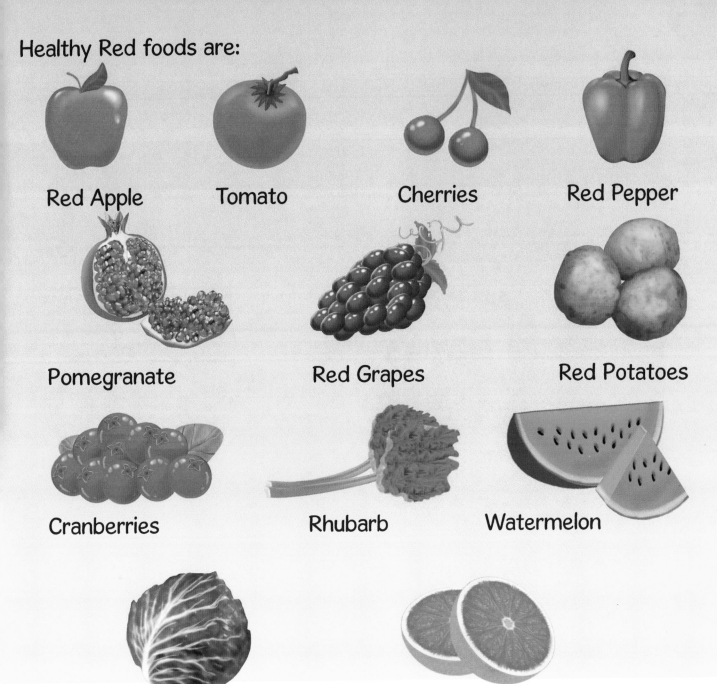

Red Apple

Tomato

Cherries

Red Pepper

Pomegranate

Red Grapes

Red Potatoes

Cranberries

Rhubarb

Watermelon

Radicchio

Pink or Red Grapefruit

I love to play outside in the sun. I will think of yellow and orange fruits and vegetables next.

Healthy Orange and Yellow foods are:

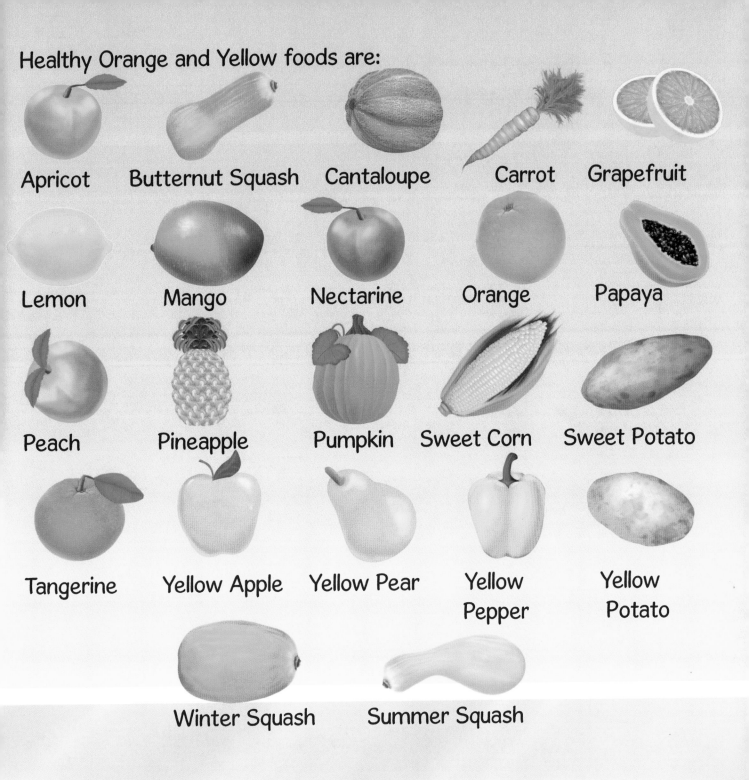

Apricot   Butternut Squash   Cantaloupe   Carrot   Grapefruit

Lemon   Mango   Nectarine   Orange   Papaya

Peach   Pineapple   Pumpkin   Sweet Corn   Sweet Potato

Tangerine   Yellow Apple   Yellow Pear   Yellow Pepper   Yellow Potato

Winter Squash   Summer Squash

My dietitian says, "You can't go wrong with green!"
I love everything green that I see outdoors.

There are so many fun green things to eat.

Healthy Green foods are:

Artichoke

Arugala

Asparagus

Avocados

Broccoli

Brussels Sprouts

Celery

Cucumber

Green Apple

Green Beans

Cabbage

Green Grapes

Green Onion

Green Pear

Green Pepper

Honeydew

Kale

Kiwi Fruit

Lettuce

Lime

Peas

Snow Peas

Spinach

Sugar Snap Peas

Zucchini

Blue sky and beautiful purple flowers remind me of these colorful fruits and vegetables.

Healthy Bluish Purple foods are:

Beet   Eggplant   Plum   Purple Cabbage

Purple Grapes   Raisins   Prunes   Bluish Plum

There are also white fruits and vegetables that are good to eat. Bananas will fool you because they are yellow on the outside and white on the inside!

Bananas   Cauliflower   Jicama

Mushrooms   Onions   Potatoes

Berries are very colorful and especially good for you. Eating them can make you smarter because they help your brain. They can help protect you from harmful diseases. Blueberries and Raspberries especially help your eyes stay healthy.

If you find a different kind of berry, be sure to check with an adult first before you eat it.

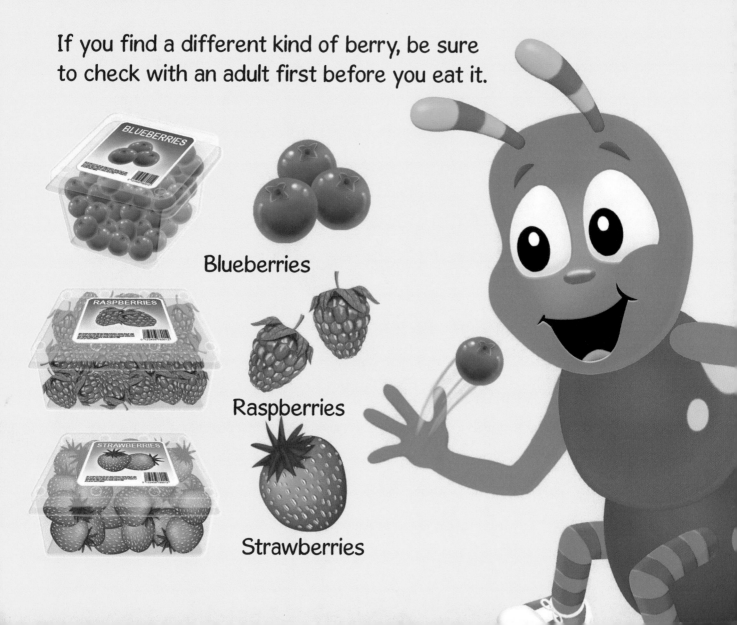

Blueberries

Raspberries

Strawberries

Beans are great to eat because they have lots of protein that your body needs to build muscles and make you stronger. There are many kinds of beans. Two of my favorites are Black beans and Garbanzo beans, sometimes known as Chickpeas, because I can add them to my salads.

Nuts are great for snacks. They have oils, proteins, and vitamins that your body needs to be healthy. A handful of Almonds or Walnuts will help keep you going throughout your day.

Drinking plenty of water will keep your body running smoothly. Water works to clean your body on the inside as well as the outside. It is best to drink water 10 to 15 minutes before or after you eat. This helps your stomach juices digest, or break up your food better.

Remember to drink water during the day and when you exercise too!

It is important to eat whole grains every day. Some good grains to eat are oatmeal, brown rice, whole wheat, and rye. Making sandwiches with whole grain breads is an easy way to get grains into your body. I love a bowl of oatmeal for breakfast. I put berries in my oatmeal for extra flavor and vitamins.

Your body also needs protein. Eggs, fish (like wild salmon), and chicken are great ways to get protein. I like scrambled eggs with vegetables and cheese in them. You can put just about any vegetable in your scrambled eggs. Vegetables, beans, nuts, seeds, and grains all have some amount of protein in them too.

Choosing five or more fruits and vegetables a day will keep your heart and body healthy.

Fruits and vegetables give our bodies vitamins, minerals, and fiber to help them work better. Juices do not usually have much fiber.

Our brains need special oils from plants, seeds, and nuts.

Eating protein will help build muscles and give us energy.

Drinking plenty of water will keep our bodies running smoothly.

Making healthy food choices will help us feel great!

I'm Sammy the Centipede.
My love for healthy eating never ends.
Now that you can eat a rainbow,
you can tell all your friends!

Your friend,
Sammy the Centipede

Recipes for you to Enjoy

with a little help from your parents

MINI PIZZA

Toast a whole grain muffin.
Put tomato sauce on first and then
sprinkle grated cheese on top.
You may also put other vegetables on top
like green or red peppers and olives.

FRESH FRUIT

Wash your favorite fruit
and have it for a nutritious snack.
Ask for help if it is the kind of fruit you need
to peel or if you need to remove a pit.

JUST BERRIES

Wash your favorite berries in a strainer.
Let them stand and drain.
Eat some now and put the rest in a plastic zip lock bag
and lay them flat on a cookie sheet in the freezer.
When they are frozen you can take them out
and eat them for a snack later.

YOGURT SMOOTHIE

Put all of these ingredients into the blender and mix.
One peeled banana
1/2 cup berries or your favorite fruit
3/4 cup of nonfat yogurt or your favorite low-fat yogurt
1 cup skim milk

WHOLE GRAIN CRACKERS AND CHEESE

Take 6 whole grain crackers and eat them
with cubes of your favorite cheese.

YOGURT WITH BERRIES

Mix fresh berries into a cup of Plain Yogurt or Greek Yogurt.

SAMMY SALAD

2 handfuls of Spinach
¼ cup of chopped walnuts
A ripe pear cut into small pieces

Toss these ingredients in a bowl and drizzle with 2 Tablespoons of
Raspberry Vinaigrette dressing or low-fat yogurt

ANYTHING GOES SALAD

Fill your favorite large bowl one-half full of lettuce.
Then, according to what you like, your parents can chop,
grate or cut up your favorite vegetables and you
can help add them to the salad.

Some suggestions are:
Tomatoes, carrots, snow peas,
celery, and purple cabbage.

You may also want to add
Black beans or chickpeas too!

Other books by Maria include:

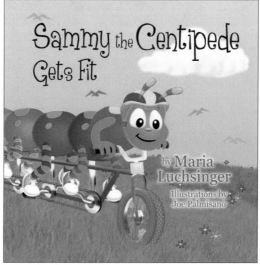

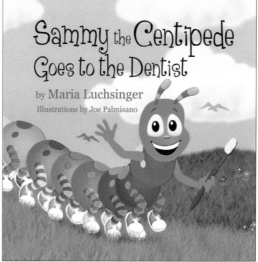

You will find
Sammy the Centipede books at
www.MariaLuchsinger.com

Acknowledgments:

I would like to thank my husband, John, and my loving family and friends for their encouragement and support.

Special thanks to the following people for their review :

Liubov S. Sichel, Ph.D.
Specializing in Probiotic Research

> "Sammy the Centipede Goes to the Market is potentially able to create a foundation for fundamental change in the food selection habits for this and future generations. This book does so by making scientifically correct information fun to learn with colorful and engaging illustrations of Sammy the Centipede. Children will love Sammy as a friend who will remind them of smart daily food choices."

Eileen Paul, RDN CD
Certified Dietitian with Washington State

> "Children love to eat good food and eat food that is good for them, especially when they help shop for it, prepare it with an adult, and understand how it helps their bodies grow. Eat a rainbow of five or more fruits and vegetables each day."

About the Author:

Maria Luchsinger is a teacher and literacy advocate who has a passion to write engaging and educational books for children.

She was awarded two scholarships on her way to graduating with honors from Central Washington University with a Bachelor of Arts in elementary education.

Contact Maria Luchsinger for more information as shown below:
Email: Maria@Marialuchsinger.com.
Twitter: @Marialuchsinger
Linked In: Maria Luchsinger
Facebook: Sammy the Centipede
Pinterest: Maria Luchsinger, Author

Made in the USA
Charleston, SC
11 April 2015